# The Sales Whisperer

*Communication Skills for Closing More Deals*

# Table of Contents

# Chapter 1. Introduction

Welcome to a definitive special report that brings out the hidden salesperson in you - 'The Sales Whisperer: Communication Skills for Closing More Deals'. This report is brimming with cheerful, practical, and proven strategies that even the most seasoned sales professionals will find invaluable. With the right blend of wisdom, humor, and actionable advice, you will be persuaded not just to buy this report, but to step your foot boldly into the rewarding world of sales! You want to close more deals? Whisper your language of sales with assurance? You are just a step away! Get ready to uncover the secrets of effective communication that will turn every 'maybe' into a 'yes, please!' in no time. Let's hustle and turn those sales targets into achievements!

# Chapter 2. Mastering the Art of Effective Listening

There's an old adage that says we have two ears and one mouth for a reason - listening is twice as important as speaking. In the world of sales, this resonates profoundly. By mastering the art of effective listening, you can decipher your customer's hidden desires, their unspoken needs, and the solutions they're seeking - all these, without your client having to utter a word.

## 2.1. The Power of Active Listening

Active listening is by far the most powerful tool in your sales armory. Anything your customer says is a clue to what they want, need, or fear. Ignoring these cues is akin to leaving money on the table.

So, what exactly is active listening? It's not just about hearing what your client says. It's about being fully engaged in the conversation, empathizing with the other person, and understanding their perspective.

Active listening involves paying attention to both verbal and non-verbal cues. These include body language, tone of voice, facial expressions, and even silences. An active listener is attentive, responsive, and open to the speaker's perspective.

## 2.2. The Art of Empathy

Empathy is foundational to effective listening. It paves the way for genuine understanding and fosters trust within your relationship.

As a salesperson, when you empathize with a client, you step into their shoes and see the world from their perspective. This understanding can help you tailor your offering to their specific needs, resulting in a win-win situation for all.

To empathize with your clients, strive to understand their emotions, motivations, and goals. Ask clarifying questions to grasp their point of view better and build deeper connections.

## 2.3. Nodding and Smiling

Active listening is not just about hearing; it's also about showing that you're hearing. A simple nod or a smile can go a long way in affirming that you're engaged and attentive.

But don't overdo it. Nodding and smiling should be a genuine reaction to what the speaker is saying, not a mechanical response.

## 2.4. Restating and Asking Questions

Restating and asking questions are two powerful techniques to ensure clarity of communication. Restating the speaker's point in your own words shows that you've comprehended their perspective, and it also provides them a chance to correct any misinterpretations.

Asking open-ended questions encourages the speaker to elaborate their thoughts and gives them the assurance that you're genuinely interested in understanding their needs and expectations.

## 2.5. The Grace of Silence

Sometimes, the best response is no response at all. Allowing silence to fill the conversation can be a powerful listening technique. It provides the speaker with the space to formulate their thoughts, choose their words, and share their feelings.

Remember, all good things take time. Your willingness to sit in silence shows your respect for the speaker's process and your commitment to understanding their perspective.

## 2.6. Practice Makes Perfect

Like any other skill, effective listening takes practice. It might feel unnatural or forced at first, but with time, it will become second nature.

Strive every day to listen more and talk less. Practice active listening with colleagues, friends, and family. The more you listen, the more you'll learn, and the better a salesperson you'll become.

Becoming an effective listener is an ongoing journey of learning and self-improvement. However, the rewards it brings – increased sales, stronger relationships, and higher customer satisfaction – make this journey truly worthwhile.

## 2.7. A Call to Action

In the end, effective listening is about creating meaningful connections. It's about building trust, fostering empathy, and making your clients feel heard.

So the next time you encounter a 'maybe', put on your listening ears, open your heart, and genuinely engage in the conversation. You'll be amazed at how quickly those 'maybes' turn into 'yes, pleases!'

Remember, your ability to listen effectively is directly proportional to your success in sales. Act now, become a master listener, and watch your sales skyrocket!

# Chapter 3. The Power of Persuasive Speech

The ability to persuade is integral to the human condition. At the core, every decision we make is a result of some level of persuasion. Whether from marketing messages, a trusted advisor's recommendation, or even our own internal thought processes, we are continually persuaded towards action. In sales, negotiation, and leadership roles, the power of persuasive speech is a vital tool—used correctly, it can turn the tide of a deal, inspiring confidence and spurring action.

## 3.1. Understanding Persuasive Speech

Persuasive speech seeks to convince, influence, or motivate an audience to adopt a belief or take a particular course of action. This happens in everyday situations such as convincing a friend to try out a new restaurant, or in business contexts like convincing clients to purchase a product or service.

In sales specifically, the power of persuasive speech allows salespeople to effectively communicate the value of a product or service, overcome objections, and push for a close. The art of persuasive speech involves blending empathy, understanding, and strategic delivery to maximize impact.

Empathy allows salespeople to connect with their audience on a human level. Analyzing prospects' needs, concerns, and interests provides meaningful insights essential for crafting a persuasive argument. Understanding, on the other hand, refers to a clear grasp of the product or service being sold. To persuade someone to take a desired action, you first need to be fully convinced of its value yourself.

Finally, strategic delivery pertains to how the argument is presented. It involves a calculated application of various persuasive techniques such as rhetorical questions, analogies, storytelling, using emotions, and practical evidence to deliver a memorable and compelling pitch.

# 3.2. The Science Behind Persuasion

On a fundamental level, people's decisions, choices, and actions are driven by six key psychological principles of persuasion identified by Dr. Robert Cialdini. These include Reciprocity, Scarcity, Authority, Consistency, Liking, and Social Proof.

1. **Reciprocity:** We feel obligated to return favors after people do something for us.
2. **Scarcity:** We place higher value on opportunities that are less available.
3. **Authority:** We tend to follow people who provide expert guidance.
4. **Consistency:** We strive to remain consistent in our beliefs and commitments.
5. **Liking:** We prefer to say yes to those we like and trust.
6. **Social Proof:** We feel more confident in making decisions when others are doing the same.

In sales, understanding and leveraging these principles can radically improve your effectiveness as a communicator and negotiator.

# 3.3. Building Rapport and Establishing Trust

Building rapport is the foundation of any successful persuasive communication. Any attempt to persuade without first having established a level of trust and mutual respect is likely to be ineffective. Actively listen, show empathy, maintain eye contact, and mirror body language. Be open, authentic, and respectful. These are simple techniques for building rapport, yet they can dramatically improve your persuasive abilities.

Establishing trust is also paramount. Integrity counts. Salespeople who act in their customer's best interest earn trust, and with it comes the added benefit of referrals and repeat business. A promising way to build trust is by delivering on your promises and showing that you value the relationship more than the sale.

# 3.4. Mastering the Art of Storytelling

Storytelling can powerfully enhance persuasive speech as it makes what you're presenting relatable and memorable. People are more likely to be persuaded when they can visualize or emotionally connect with a scenario.

Effective storytelling requires integrating convincing details within a coherent and engaging narrative. Encapsulate the benefits of your product, celebrate your company's victories, or personify your brand's journey in a compelling narrative. Importantly, your customer should always be the central character with whom the audience can identify.

## 3.5. Combining Logic and Emotion in Speech

Successful persuasive speech depends on striking a balance between appealing to logic and evoking emotion. Rational arguments build cognitive conviction by using evidence, logical reasoning, and proof points to demonstrate the merits of your case. Emotive language, meanwhile, creates a feeling, stimulant, or image that helps to elicit an emotional response.

When these two elements are successfully combined in a persuasive speech, audiences are more likely to act because they're not just intellectually convinced but emotionally engaged as well.

## 3.6. Speaking with Authority and Confidence

People are more likely to be persuaded by someone who speaks with authority and confidence. An authoritative speaker establishes credibility, demonstrates expertise, and commands respect.

There are many strategies to enhance your authority and confidence: thorough knowledge of your industry, articulating ideas clearly, providing solutions, showing credibility through accomplishments and testimonials, using a confident tone, maintaining assertive body language, and responding to objections professionally and factually.

## 3.7. Summarizing for Impact

Summarizations are powerful tools of persuasive speaking. By summarizing key points at strategic moments, you can remind your audience about the benefits and opportunities that your offering presents. Done successfully, it leaves your audience with emotional high points and consensus-building arguments.

Persuasion is an art that requires thoughtful application, practice, and refinement. Mastering persuasive speech is not just about selling better; it's about communicating better, building stronger relationships, and leading more effectively. That's the power of persuasive speech. If you can wield it, in even the most challenging situations, you'll find doors swinging open, opportunities falling into place, and, usually, just the outcome you're looking for. Use these tactics and strategies wisely; your words have the power to transform not just your sales, but your entire career trajectory.

The journey of mastering persuasive speech requires consistent learning and adaptation. The more you understand people and the art of persuasion, the more you'll grow as a salesperson. Embrace this challenge and watch your sales numbers soar. Remember, each no only brings you closer to a yes, but it's also an opportunity to learn, grow, and perfect your art of persuasion.

# Chapter 4. Understand Your Customer's Persona

Understanding your customer's persona is fundamental to the sales process; it is the crucible where excellent salespeople forge their strategies. This process requires one to delve into the psyche, behavior, and preferences of the prospect; thereby equipping the salesperson with the robust toolkit needed to close deals with seamless precision.

## 4.1. Why Knowing Your Customer Matters

Firstly, let us decrypt why honing this understanding is imperative. A sales pitch can either sound like a monotonous drone or a harmonious symphony; the distinction is made by how well you tailor your message towards your customer's persona. When you truly understand your customer, you can meticulously align your offering to meet their identified needs, leading to higher conversion rates, shorter sales cycle, and improved customer loyalty and satisfaction.

The importance of knowing your customer seeps into your sales methodology like a watermark, subtly visible, yet immensely impactful. It allows you to navigate with ease through the labyrinth that is the sales process, resulting in higher customer retention and augmenting the overall customer journey to an experience your customer likely didn't anticipate, but certainly enjoyed.

# 4.2. Individual's Unique Needs and Preferences

Everyone wears a different pair of spectacles; they perceive the world around them uniquely, influenced by their personal experiences, preferences, pain points, and aspirations. This understanding brings to the fore the need to recognize your customer's uniqueness.

Remember, in sales, one size rarely, if ever, fits all. As such, each customer walkthrough should be accompanied by different tunes, and in understanding your customer's unique needs and preferences, you are essentially arming yourself with the needed notes to compose the right sales anthem.

Let's consider an example: an environmental enthusiast and a tech aficionado unlikely have the same preferences when purchasing a car. The former may lean towards an eco-friendly model, whereas the latter could be enticed by the latest technology additions. As a salesperson, your interactions would be more meaningful if you align your pitch with their underlining interests.

Therefore, consider fitting into their shoes for a while and once you step out of them, you will have valuable tidbits to include in your tailored sales presentation.

# 4.3. Creating a Buyer Persona

The process of understanding a customer begins with creating a buyer persona, a detailed description of your ideal customer. This includes demographic information, goals, challenges, interests, among other characteristics.

A comprehensive buyer persona is akin to studying the anatomy of your customer – the better you understand it, the easier it gets to propose a solution your potential buyer can't refuse. Creating such a persona requires qualitative and quantitative data gleaned from various sources like customer surveys, interviews, social media, and CRM data.

A step-by-step process to create a buyer persona might look something like this:

1. Gather Data: Start by collecting demographic and geographical data. This could include age, profession, income, location, etc.

2. Identify Goals and Challenges: Dig deeper to understand what motivates these people. What are their aspirations? What pain points do they face?

3. Study Interactions and Preferences: What are their habits when it comes to decision-making? How do they interact with brands? Do they prefer reading blogs or watching videos?

4. Refine: After initial analysis, distill the data for better precision and more reliable personas.

# 4.4. Customer Persona Application

Having built your customer persona, it's now time to weave that knowledge into your sales fabric. For instance, if your buyer persona is likely to spend considerable time on social platforms, applying social selling techniques could strike the right chord.

Again, the customer persona should significantly influence your sales pitch. Craft your pitch in a language your persona understands and appreciates, infused with the right proportion of professionalism and amicability.

Remember that the purpose of building a customer persona is to maximize your chances of making every interaction with the customer resonant, engaging, and ultimately successful. Every cog in your communication wheel, be it verbal, non-verbal, written, or visual, should synchronize perfectly with your understanding of the customer persona.

# 4.5. Conclusion

In essence, understanding your customer's persona is like looking into a mirror, except the reflection staring back at you isn't your own – it is your customer's. Merely observing that reflection isn't sufficient; you need to investigate, understand, and empathize with it to facilitate an impactful sales conversation.

Remember, a customer well-understood is a sale nearly closed. Turn whispers into cheers, maybe into yes, uncertainty into assent, by first knowing your customers, and then knowing them some more. Let understanding their persona be your first success story in the captivating narrative that is sales.

With the right insight, approach, and hardcore perseverance, you will soon transition from just being a salesperson to a trusted consultant in the eyes of your customers. Understanding their persona is the key to unlocking the door to this highly rewarding world of sales.

# Chapter 5. Breaking Down Complex Sales Terminology

Sales. A universe filled with unique lingo and complex terminologies that can puzzle even the most veteran listener. It's a language spoken by millions, yet understood by only a select few. But worry not, for this arcane lexicon is about to get a whole lot simpler. Let's stick your cryptex into the heart of sales' complex dialect and crack open its mysteries.

Before we start breaking down complex sales terminologies, a gentle word of caution. The terms discussed herein are filled with nuanced interpretations that change from industry to industry, company to company, and even deal to deal. Take what you read here as a general guide and always modify to suit your specific context.

## 5.1. Part 1: Lead Generation Terminologies

1. **Lead:** Let's start simple. A lead is any individual or organization who might be interested in what you're selling. They may have shown interest by signing up for a newsletter, liking a social media post or merely visiting your website.

2. **Prospect:** Things get a bit heated up here as terminologies begin to overlap. A lead becomes a prospect once it's determined they meet the qualifying criteria for your product or service. Criteria could range from budget to need or even timing.

3. **Marketing Qualified Lead (MQL):** This is a lead deemed more likely to become a customer compared to other leads, based on lead intelligence. These prospects have engaged with your marketing team and shown interest, but have not yet met the criteria to become sales qualified.

4. **Sales Qualified Lead (SQL):** An MQL becomes an SQL once they've shown buying intent. For example, they have requested a demo or a meeting with the sales team or expressed an interest in buying within a specific time frame.

**Table 1. Lead Generation Terminologies**

| Term | Definition |
| --- | --- |
| Lead | Any individual or organization who might be interested in what you're selling. |
| Prospect | A lead becomes a prospect once it's determined they meet the qualifying criteria for your product or service. |
| Marketing Qualified Lead (MQL) | This is a lead deemed more likely to become a customer compared to other leads, based on lead intelligence. |
| Sales Qualified Lead (SQL) | An MQL becomes an SQL once they've shown buying intent. |

# 5.2. Part 2: Sales Pipeline Terminologies

1. **Sales Pipeline:** This is a visual representation of where prospects are in the buying process. Your sales process could have stages like "lead generation", "prospect qualification", "proposal", amongst others.

2. **Sales Funnel:** This is another representation of the buying process but with the added visualization of narrowing down from a large number of leads to a few paying customers. It's

called a 'funnel' because you start with a large base of captured leads which eventually narrows down to a steady stream of customers.

3. **Conversion Rate:** This is the percentage of prospective customers who complete a specific action you desire, be it subscribing to a newsletter, downloading a whitepaper or making a purchase.

**Table 2. Sales Pipeline Terminologies**

| Term | Definition |
| --- | --- |
| Sales Pipeline | A visual representation of where prospects are in the buying process. |
| Sales Funnel | This represents the buying process with the visualization of narrowing down from a large number of leads to a few paying customers. |
| Conversion Rate | This is the percentage of prospective customers who complete a specific action. |

# 5.3. Part 3: Sales Metrics Terminologies

1. **Customer Acquisition Cost (CAC):** This is the cost of convincing a potential customer to buy a product or service. It includes costs associated with research, marketing, accessibility and more.

2. **Customer Lifetime Value (CLTV):** This is the average amount of revenue a user brings to your business during the time they remain a customer.

3. **Average Deal Value:** This is the average revenue you get from each closed deal.

**Table 3. Sales Metrics Terminologies**

| Term | Definition |
| --- | --- |
| Customer Acquisition Cost (CAC) | This is the cost of convincing a potential customer to buy a product or service. |
| Customer Lifetime Value (CLTV) | The average amount of revenue a user brings to your business during their lifetime. |
| Average Deal Value | The average revenue you get from each closed deal. |

Deciphering the complex language of sales is a little like taking apart an intricate puzzle. It's challenging, but with patience and the right strategies, you can learn to navigate this intricate labyrinth. Understanding this terminology forms the foundation to communicate effectively with clients, team members and in comprehending your sales reports. Now, equipped with this knowledge, you can effectively converse, negotiate, and most importantly, close sales with confidence. Remember, every 'no' is just a 'yes' waiting to happen. Keep on hustling, and soon you will speak the language of sales like a true sales whisperer.

# Chapter 6. Building Trust and Rapport: A Two-Way Street

Trust and rapport are two critical components of any great salesperson's arsenal. When manipulating these in the sales process, one is saying to the customer, "Hello, I'm here to help." To ensure that these elements are genuinely perceived and beneficial, there must be an organic blend of honesty, power, and elegantly amplified communication skills.

## 6.1. The Power of Trust

The foundation for any prosperity in sales is trust. As humans, we regularly base our decisions on the degree of trust we have in the other party, and that amounts to a lot in the field of selling. When trust is given or gained, sales become a smooth process filled with less friction and resistance.

To build this level of trust, a salesperson has to exhibit reliability, competence, honesty, and a deep sense of understanding towards the client's needs and wants. Offering solutions that consistently meet or surpass the client's expectations, presenting products or services with complete accuracy, and avoiding the temptation to oversell all foster trust.

Beyond direct sales interactions, actively demonstrating your commitment to a client's success can also nurture trust. This includes effort invested in after-sales service, regular check-ins to understand changing needs, and acting as a credible resource for industry trends and information.

## 6.2. Riding High on Rapport

Rapport, although frequently interchanged with trust, is a subtly different tool in the sales process. It involves establishing a mutual understanding or emotional connection between two parties. The rapport makes dealing with each other smooth and enjoyable.

Building rapport involves respecting and understanding your client's opinions, actively offering empathy, and getting your client comfortable talking about their needs and wants. Building rapport helps to generate feelings of commonalities, leading to benefits like loyalty and repeat business.

There are various ways to create rapport: understand your client's interests, use body language effectively to show interest and attentiveness, employ humor where appropriate, and be genuinely interested in the client as a person and their needs as a customer.

## 6.3. The Loop of Reciprocity

The concept of reciprocity is surprisingly powerful in sales relationships. Simply put, the more you give, the more you get back. And in this process, one creates a highly functional, mutually beneficial model for a sales relationship.

In practice, you might be providing your customers with valuable resources and insights related to their industry, connecting them with people who can help meet their needs, or simply making their lives easier with reliable and efficient service. In return, the trust and rapport you gain can lead to increased sales and customer loyalty.

## 6.4. Practice Makes Perfect

Building trust and rapport isn't an overnight process, nor does it occur by chance. You need to be consistently honest, reliable, empathetic, and helpful. You also need to demonstrate an understanding of your customer's needs and continually strive to meet or exceed them.

Through practice, seeking feedback from clients, and continual learning, you can significantly improve your ability to build trust and rapport.

# 6.5. Conclusion: A Journey, Not a Destination

In the end, building trust and rapport should be viewed as a journey rather than a destination. Each interaction presents a new opportunity to build upon these elements and foster deeper and more meaningful relationships with your customers. It's not about making a single sale, but rather about cultivating relationships that lead to repeated business and loyalty.

Remember, your integrity, how genuinely you understand the customer's needs, and how effectively you bridge the gap between their needs and your product or service, determine your success rate as a salesperson. Let trust and rapport be your guiding forces as you communicate your way into closing more deals!

# Chapter 7. Overcoming Objection: How to Turn 'No' into 'Yes'

The art of overcoming objections is as old as sales itself. It's a critical part of any sales process, whether you're selling a product, service, or idea. But how can you turn a 'no' into a 'yes'? Start by understanding why objections arise and learn to see them not as roadblocks but as bridges to favorable solutions for both sides.

## 7.1. Understanding Objections

Objections usually happen when a prospective client is unsure, requires more information, or doesn't see a compelling value in what's being offered. The key is to not view objections as personal rejections. Instead, welcome them as opportunities to explore your client's concerns more deeply and provide them the information they need to feel more comfortable moving forward.

Step into their shoes and empathize with their concerns. Ask clarifying questions to delve into the root of their reluctance. What are they unsure about? What additional info do they need? How can you make them see the value of your product or service in a light most beneficial to them?

## 7.2. Artful Responses to Common Objections

A large part of overcoming objections involves honing your responses to the common ones. Here, we will delve into a few typical objections and the most effective ways to handle them:

- **It's too expensive.** In response to this objection, highlight the entire value your product/service offers. Don't just talk about price. Ask the prospect about the cost of not solving the problem your product/service fixes.

- **I don't have time.** Here, try asking the prospect about the time they may waste without your solution. Show how your product/service can actually save them time in the long run.

- **We are already working with someone else.** For this objection, emphasize the uniqueness of your product/service and how it differentiates from others in the market.

In tackling these common objections, remember that you are not manipulating the prospect, but offering them a perspective they might not have previously considered.

# 7.3. Embracing the LAER Method

The LAER method —an acronym for Listen, Acknowledge, Explore, Respond— is a valuable tool in swiftly dealing with objections.

Listen attentively to your prospect's concerns. Acknowledge their objections without being dismissive. Explore their issues by asking open-ended questions. And finally, respond in a thorough yet concise manner that addresses the objections directly. This method encourages effective dialogues and assists in building trust between you and your potential clients.

# 7.4. The Power of Validation

When someone objects to something, their principal concern isn't always with the objection they rise but with feeling understood. It's crucial to validate your prospect's feelings and concerns. Never dismiss an objection, or you risk your prospect feeling unheard or overlooked. Begin your responses with phrases like, "I understand where you're coming from..." or "It makes sense you'd feel that way..." Then smoothly transition into providing a suitable solution or counter-argument.

# 7.5. The Magic of Persistence

Persistence is vital in overcoming objections, but it's also important to know when to hold back. Contrary to the popular belief of 'always be closing', a smart salesperson knows when to step back and give the prospect space to think, reassess, and reciprocate.

In conclusion, overcoming objections is a delicate dance between hearing out your prospective client's concerns, addressing them effectively, and persisting sans coming off as pushy. It's an essential, intricate talent one must possess in the sales world. But once mastered, it becomes a potent weapon in turning 'no' into 'yes', taking you to stellar heights in your sales career.

# Chapter 8. Strategies for Crafting Compelling Sales Narratives

A sales narrative isn't just about showcasing your product or service; it's about attaching your offering to a story that resonates with your prospects. In essence, it's a means of demonstrating ideal situations where your product would come into play and save the day. With a compelling narrative, you build a bridge of empathy, connecting your audience's needs with your value proposition.

## 8.1. Building the Foundation of Your Sales Narrative

Before you get into the intricacies of the narrative, it's critical to prepare the groundwork. This foundation enables a stepping stone that supports your narrative and amplifies the weight of your words.

Dominant themes include: * The Problem: Highlight the pain points faced by your potential customers. The problem forms the core of your narrative because it sets the stage where your product or service becomes relevant. * The Solution: After highlighting the problem, bring forth your solution. Be careful not to delve into the specifics too soon; instead, provide a general overview of how your product or service addresses the problem. * The Application: Use real-life scenarios or situations to demonstrate how your solution works in action.

## 8.2. The Art of Storytelling in Sales

Storytelling is not a domain exclusive to writers and filmmakers; it is important in the world of sales as well. Narratives infused with the right details and emotions make any offering more relatable.

To master the art of storytelling in sales: * Understand Your Prospect: Your narrative should revolve around your prospective buyer. Understand their needs, frustrations, desires, and aspirations. Make it about them, not you. * Be Authentic: In trying to make your narrative compelling, don't stray far from the truth. Fabricated stories might intrigue your audience initially but will eventually lead to mistrust and skepticism. * Add Human Elements: We humans are wired to connect with human elements - emotions, struggles, triumphs. These elements bring authenticity and emotional appeal, adding soul to your narrative.

## 8.3. Leveraging Empathy in Your Sales Narrative

Empathy is understanding and sharing another person's feelings, and it is a powerful tool in crafting compelling sales narratives.

To leverage empathy: * Listen More, Speak Less: True empathy begins with listening - understanding your prospect's position. The more you listen, the easier it will be to tell a story that resonates. * Share Experiences: Sharing experiences is another tactical way of showing that you understand what your prospects are going through. It builds a bridge of connectivity, making the prospect feel seen and heard.

## 8.4. Techniques to Optimize Your Sales Narrative

After crafting the narrative, it's time to refine and optimize it for maximum impact. Here are a few techniques to polish your sales story: * Simplicity: Keep your narrative simple, clear, and compelling.

Remember, you are not writing a novel here; the focus should be on addressing the pain points. * Consistency: A consistent narrative is easier to follow and believe. Ensure that each part of your story connects to the next logically, forming a cohesive whole. * Use Cases: Use cases help prospects visualize, understand, and believe in your solution. By painting a clear picture of how your product or service can improve their situation, you engender trust and credibility. * Testimonials: Incorporate customer testimonials into your narrative. It's one thing to say you can solve a problem; it's another to prove indeed you have done so before.

# 8.5. Inculcating a Sense of Urgency in Your Sales Narrative

A sense of urgency compels action. It shifts the prospect from consideration to decision, making them more likely to close the deal.

To inculcate a sense of urgency: * Show the Consequences: What happens if the problem you're solving for continues without your solution? Highlight the implications clearly to instill a sense of urgent action. * Create Limited Offers: Limited offers - discounts, bonuses, or freebies - that are time-bound can create a sense of urgency. It nudges the prospect to act before the offer runs out, helping you close the deal faster.

In conclusion, crafting compelling sales narratives is a continual process of understanding your customers, sculpting your story around their pain points, refining your narrative for clarity and consistency, and adding elements that drive action. With these strategies, you put yourself in a prime position to close more sales, gain trust, and create long-term customer relationships. Remember, people don't buy products - they buy better versions of themselves. Your sales narrative is a bridge that connects their current state with that improved version, and the better you build this bridge, the more deals you close.

# Chapter 9. Non-Verbal Communication in Sales: The Hidden Language

Just as in everyday life, the way we communicate in sales extends beyond the words we use. Our non-verbal cues, including body language, facial expressions, tone, and gestures, carry a large chunk of our message, often revealing more about our intentions than words alone. It's the silent, subconscious language that speaks volumes. In sales, learning to understand and use this language can be the key to closing that challenging deal.

## 9.1. The Colossal Influence of Non-Verbal Communication

Non-verbal communication encompasses all the ways we transmit information without words. Its power overrides verbal communication, playing a dominant role in how our messages are interpreted. Recent studies suggest that non-verbal cues account for almost 70% of communication, making them an invaluable tool in the sales process.

Understanding the non-verbal cues of your potential clients can provide insight into their comfort level, interest, confusion, or hesitation. Similarly, being conscious about the non-verbal signals you send can help build trust, positively influence perceptions, and reinforce your message.

## 9.2. Recognizing Non-Verbal Cues in a Client

As a salesperson, you communicate with diverse clients, each with unique expressions and body reactions. Therefore, paying attention to their non-verbal cues can provide crucial information. After all, a client refusing eye contact, constantly looking at the watch, or having tight body language might indicate disinterest or an urgency to end the meeting.

Learning to recognize these cues is your first step towards effective non-verbal communication. Beside eye contact, focus on the direction their body is facing, personal space, facial expressions, and any repetitive movement. Be conscious about their breathing and voice patterns during the conversation.

## 9.3. Postural Messages

Posture is a powerful component of non-verbal language in sales. An open, relaxed posture implies interest and willingness for the conversation. Contrarily, a closed posture - crossed arms, hunched shoulders, legs crossed away from you - might indicate disinterest, discomfort, or disagreement.

Your posture also communicates your feelings and attitudes. Leaning in subtly while the client is talking can signal your keen attention. Maintaining an upright and balanced posture communicates confidence, suggesting reliability and professionalism.

## 9.4. Mastering the Eye Language

Eyes can disclose much about a person's internal state during a conversation. They're also sensitive to the behavior of those around them. Steady eye contact demonstrates interest, honesty, and receptivity. It assures the client that you're present and focused. However, maintain a balanced approach - excessively intense eye contact can come off as aggressive or intrusive.

Look for changes in pupil size, eye glance patterns, and frequency of blinking. These cues can reveal curiosity, nervousness, or potential disagreement. Incorporate pauses to break the eye contact politely, aiding comfort for both parties.

# 9.5. Winning Smiles and Facial Expressions

A genuine smile can transform a sales interaction, conveying warmth, understanding, and openness. It can make your client feel valued and comfortable, fostering a positive atmosphere.

Beyond smiles, your facial expressions should match your words. Express surprise, concern, or excitement as appropriate. However, ensure your expressions are genuine as forced emotions can seem insincere, causing more harm than good.

# 9.6. The Handshake: A Silent Introduction

The handshake can initiate trust, setting the tone for the rest of the conversation. Aim for a firm, but not tight, handshake. Eye contact and a warm smile during the handshake also indicate sincerity and interest.

# 9.7. Personal Space and Territoriality

Appreciating personal space is an essential part of non-verbal communication. Invading personal space can make others uncomfortable. Maintain a respectful distance - close enough to engage, yet far enough to avoid discomfort.

# 9.8. Decoding Voice Cues

The way you speak - your pitch, quality of voice, volume, and speed - can significantly impact the interpretation of your message. Similarly, the client's vocal cues can express their comfort, disagreement, excitement or dullness.

A warm, friendly voice can help establish rapport. However, quick, loud speech may signal nervousness, while a slow, low pitch can suggest lack of interest or confidence.

# 9.9. Case Study: Applying Non-Verbal Communication Techniques

Let's bring these principles to life with a case study. Consider John, a sales representative, meeting with a potential client, Mr. Taylor for the first time. John starts with a firm, warm handshake, maintaining eye contact and a friendly smile. Throughout the meeting, he observes Mr. Taylor's body language - the way he leans in when interested, shifts away when uncomfortable, and his altered tone when discussing budget.

John adapts his behavior, slowing down when Mr. Taylor shows signs of confusion and mirroring the positive gestures. His ability to read and respond to non-verbal cues ensures he effectively addresses Mr.

Taylor's concerns, soothes his fears, and closes the deal.

In conclusion, mastering non-verbal communication can be a game-changer in sales. By being conscious of your body language and tuning into the client's non-verbal cues, you create a trustful atmosphere, convey your message convincingly and increase your chances of closing deals. In the end, it is not just about what you say, but how you say it!

# Chapter 10. Emotion-Centric Selling: Capitalizing on the Feel-Good Factor

Today's consumers are smart. They are no longer swayed by cold information or generic sales pitches. Instead, they desire personalized experiences and emotional connections with brands. This emphasizes the importance of unleashing the power of emotion-centric selling, using positive emotional engagement to make your service or product irresistible. But how do you do it? This is the question we will answer in this portion of the report.

## 10.1. The Power of Emotion in Selling

The reality is that people make purchasing decisions based on emotions and justify them later using facts. A study by the Advertising Research Foundation found that the 'likeability' of an advertisement is the most powerful driver of sales. And what makes something 'likable'? The emotion it evokes.

In a remarkable study conducted by neuroscientist Antonio Damasio, patients with damage to the part of the brain where emotions are generated were unable to make even the smallest decisions like what to eat. Their thinking and reasoning abilities were intact, but without emotion, they couldn't choose.

Emotions are not just related to personal life but get carried forward into professional decisions as well. As salespersons, we can strategically incorporate them into our selling process, transforming it into an experience customers cherish.

## 10.2. Crafting Emotionally Intelligent Sales Pitches

It all begins with connection. Crafting an emotionally intelligent sales pitch starts with understanding your clients. What is their unique perspective? What are their fears, problems, and desires? Once you know these, your products or services can be positioned as the solutions they are looking for, tapping into the emotions that your prospective customers feel.

Remember the beauty of a sale is in its individuality. No two customers are the same. Hence, customized solutions not only send the message of 'I understand you' but also 'I value you'. This helps foster trust, appeal to emotions, and eventually makes way for increased sales.

Observe your client's facial expressions, tone of voice, and body language during discussions. These cues provide an insight into their emotional state and help in adjusting your selling approach.

## 10.3. Stories Sell

There is an old saying in sales: "Facts tell, but stories sell." A good storyteller can evoke an emotional response, engaging listeners, and providing a relatable context for the product or service. Whenever possible, use narratives that resonate with your customers. Tell them about other clients who were in similar situations and benefited from your offerings. Allow them to imagine the change they can experience.

When sharing a story, emphasize the feelings involved. Was your previous client ecstatic when their problem was solved? Was there a sense of relief? By focusing on the emotional aspect, you can make a strong connection with your customers and make them more willing to buy.

# 10.4. Harnessing Emotional Triggers

Each customer has unique emotional triggers - understanding and leveraging these can lead to successful sales. The most common triggers include aspiration (the desire to achieve), fear (the anxiety of missing out), and belonging (the need to fit in). If you can identify these triggers and highlight how your product or service caters to them, you are bound to make an impact.

Always follow up your pitches by asking customers how they feel about your offerings. Are they excited? Anxious? This feedback can assist you in refining your future sales strategy.

# 10.5. The Fine Line Between Empathy and Sympathy

As salespersons, there is a crucial difference between empathy and sympathy that we must understand. Sympathy makes us feel sorry for clients while empathy means understanding them. In sales, empathy trumps sympathy. Take time to understand your customers' challenges and walk them through how your products can solve their issues.

So, remember to evoke emotions, but in a way that emphasizes with your potential customers' situation while highlighting the benefits your product offers. This balanced approach is likely to engage customers on an emotional level, propelling the chances of a successful sale.

The realm of emotion-centric selling awaits; are you ready to set foot in it? You can make an emotional connection at any point in the selling process. Just believe in your product, and the rest will follow. Remember, the best salesperson doesn't just sell a product or service, but an experience filled with emotions. With the power of positive emotional engagement, every 'no' becomes just another step closer to 'yes'.

# Chapter 11. The Magic of Follow-Up: Don't Drop the Ball After Closing

Successful sales lie not just in closing a deal but in the follow up that ensues. Once you've shaken hands and signed contracts, the real work begins. The road to long-term customer relationships and repeat business is paved with consistent, persistent, and thoughtful follow-ups.

## 11.1. The Art of Effective Follow-Up

While follow up can seem tedious, especially after a successful close, it's an important tool to maintain communication, show appreciation, and lay the groundwork for future sales opportunities. Truly effective follow up is the difference between a one-time sale and a lifetime customer. Timing, persistence, personalization, and relevance are the key components to mastering the art of follow up.

Timing is imperative; too soon and you risk seeming pushy, too late and the customer may feel neglected. The sweet spot is anywhere between 24 to 48 hours after the deal has been closed. This gives the customer enough time to reflect on the sale but still keeps you fresh in their mind.

Persistence pays off. Don't be discouraged if you don't get a response immediately. Be patient and consistent. Follow up until you get a response but tread carefully to not cross into the territory of annoyance or desperation.

Personalized follow-up shows that you value the customer as an individual and appreciate their unique needs and wants. Generic, cookie-cutter messages lack authenticity and resonate less with customers.

Relevance is crucial in follow-up communications. Always bring something new or beneficial to the table. Your follow-ups should add value, be it in the form of new product information, industry updates, or additional services they might find useful.

## 11.2. The Power of Thank You

Never underestimate the power of a simple 'thank you.' Thanking your client for their business shows appreciation, fosters goodwill, and builds positive rapport. Thanking a client is the first step in converting a first-time buyer into a repeat customer. This approach is not old-fashioned or outdated but instead, a time-tested method that works.

## 11.3. Keep Adding Value

Show the client that you're not just interested in the transaction but in an ongoing relationship. Keep them informed about future deals, discounts, or events. If a new product comes to market that you think they would be interested in, reach out. The aim is to build a rapport where you are their go-to person for any purchases within your niche.

## 11.4. Customer Feedback

Collecting customer feedback is crucial for understanding how your products or services are performing post-sale. It not only helps you gain insights into customer satisfaction levels but also provides an opportunity to rectify any issues, showing your customers that you genuinely care.

## 11.5. Building Long-Term Relationships

Regular follow-ups help in building long-term relationships with your clients. The secret to maintaining these relationships is staying in the forefront of your customer's mind, without being intrusive. A helpful tip, a relevant conversation, or just a check-in call can go a long way.

## 11.6. Nurturing the Relationship through Social Media

In the era of digital connectivity, social media presents a unique opportunity to keep the conversation going with your customers. Social networks make it easy to stay connected with your clients, share updates on new products, industry trends, and provide a platform for customer interaction.

Follow-ups should not be looked upon as a mundane task, rather it is an essential part of the sales process. The key is to view it as an opportunity and use it skillfully to build a lasting relationship, retain clients, generate repeat business, and find new opportunities. So, don't drop the ball after closing; juggle it with finesse and keep the sales momentum going. Put these strategies into action and watch your customer relationships and repeat sales figures soar. Remember, the magic truly lies in the follow-up!

(Note: This is a brief overview and would need to be expanded to meet a 5 A4 page requirement. You could delve in-depth into each of these subtopics, share stories, and include more specific strategies/tactics related to your business or industry.)